Egypt

by Rachel Anne Cantor

Consultant: Marjorie Faulstich Orellana, PhD
Professor of Urban Schooling
University of California, Los Angeles

BEARPORT
PUBLISHING

New York, New York

Credits

Cover, © Dan Breckwoldt/Shutterstock and © Africa Studio/Shutterstock; TOC, © Leoks/Shutterstock; 4, © Pius Lee/Dreamstime; 5L, © B. O'Kane/Alamy; 5R, © Greg Balfour Evans/Alamy; 7, © Efesenko/iStock; 8, © hadynyah/iStock; 9, © Mayerberg/iStock; 10, © Divesh_Mistry/iStock; 11T, © Pat P/Shutterstock; 11B, © Hemis/Alamy; 12, © The Print Collector/Alamy; 13T, © Lu Yang/Shutterstock; 13B, © Heritage Image Partnership Ltd/Alamy; 14–15, © WitR/Shutterstock; 15R, © Pius Lee/Shutterstock; 16L, © James May/Alamy; 16–17, © Associated Press; 18, © NourElRefai/iStock; 19, © ONEWORLD PICTURE/Alamy; 20, © Sabena Jane Blackbird/Alamy; 21, © Shehzad Noorani/Majority World/AGE Fotostock; 22, © PHILIPPE ROYER/Sagaphoto /AGE Fotostock; 23, © Poznyakov/Shutterstock; 24, © Daniel M. Cisilino/Dreamstime; 25T, © Zurijeta/Shutterstock; 25B, © Sirirak/iStock; 26, © Egyptian Studio/Shutterstock; 27T, © DronG/Shutterstock; 27B, © hadynyah/iStock; 28, © Shehzad Noorani/Majority World/AGE Fotostock; 29, © CHEN WS/Shutterstock; 30T, © Daniel Wiedemann/Shutterstock and © Fat Jackey/Shutterstock; 30B, © Kenishirotie/Shutterstock; 31 (T to B), © Leonid Andronov/Shutterstock, © Netfalls/Dreamstime, © Hang Dinh/Shutterstock, and © Jakub Kyncl/Shutterstock; 32, © YANGCHAO/Shutterstock.

Publisher: Kenn Goin
Senior Editor: Joyce Tavolacci
Creative Director: Spencer Brinker
Design: Debrah Kaiser
Photo Researcher: Thomas Persano

Library of Congress Cataloging-in-Publication Data

Names: Cantor, Rachel Anne, author.
Title: Egypt / by Rachel Anne Cantor.
Description: New York, New York : Bearport Publishing Company, Inc., 2018. |
  Series: Countries we come from | Includes bibliographical references and
  index.
Identifiers: LCCN 2017039216 (print) | LCCN 2017039838 (ebook) |
  ISBN 9781684025312 (ebook) | ISBN 9781684024735 (library)
Subjects: LCSH: Egypt—Juvenile literature.
Classification: LCC DT49 (ebook) | LCC DT49 .C36 2018 (print) | DDC 962—dc23
LC record available at https://lccn.loc.gov/2017039216

For more information, write to Bearport Publishing Company, Inc., 45 West 21st Street, Suite 3B, New York, New York 10010. Printed in the United States of America.

10 9 8 7 6 5 4 3 2 1

Contents

This Is Egypt

ANCIENT

MODERN

Beautiful

Egypt is a country in North Africa.
More than 97 million people
live there.

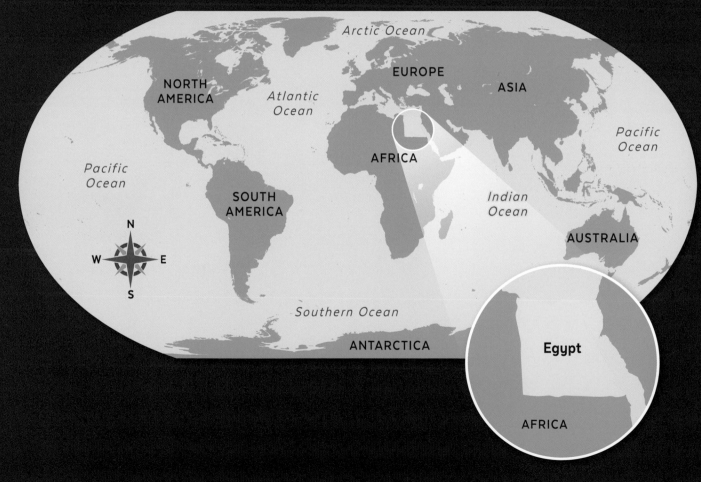

The country's full name is
the Arab Republic of Egypt.

Most of Egypt's land is dry, sandy desert.

A long river called the Nile flows through the country.

Around it, the land is green and lush.

The Nile River is 4,258 miles (6,853 km) long. It's the second-longest river in the world!

9

Crocodiles lurk at the Nile River's edge.

Nile crocodiles can grow up to 20 feet (6 m) long! That's about as long as a pickup truck.

Graceful gazelles roam the desert.

Dorcas gazelle

Cobras slither along the ground.

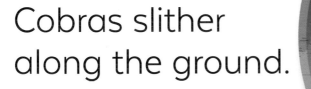

Egyptian cobra

Egypt has a very long history.

The country is home to one of the world's oldest **civilizations**.

The ancient Egyptians lived around 2,500 to 5,000 years ago!

People in
ancient Egypt
built great
cities.

They also made
beautiful art.

Egypt is famous for its ancient pyramids.

The huge stone structures were built as royal **tombs**.

The ancient Egyptians also built the Sphinx. It's a stone figure with a human head on a lion's body!

In modern times, different groups have controlled Egypt.

In the 1880s, England ruled the country.

The Egyptians fought for their own government.

In 1952, Egypt became a free country.

In 2011, there was a **revolution** in Egypt. The people wanted a new leader.

Egyptians celebrating their freedom in 1952

17

The **capital** of Egypt is Cairo.
It's also the country's
biggest city.

More than 18 million people live in Cairo.

Egyptian Arabic is the main language in Egypt.

This is how you say *thank you* in Egyptian Arabic:

Šukran (SHOOK-ran)

This is how you say *sorry*:

Āsif (AH-seef)

The ancient Egyptians used **hieroglyphic** writing. It uses pictures to represent things and sounds.

a classroom in Egypt

21

What sport do Egyptians love?

Soccer!

People also like to play squash.

They use rackets to hit a ball against a wall.

Nour El Sherbini is a famous Egyptian squash champion.

Religion is important to many Egyptians.

Most people are Muslim.

They worship in places called mosques.

Ramadan is a month-long Muslim holiday.

People eat and drink only after sunset.

Muslims hang colorful lanterns in their homes during Ramadan.

Yum! Egyptians cook tasty meals.

Aish baladi (EYESH bah-LAH-dee) is a puffy bread.

Kofta kebabs are chunks of meat cooked on a stick.

In Egyptian cooking, spices add flavor to food. Cinnamon and cumin are often used.

Egypt is a popular place to visit.
More than 14 million tourists
go there each year!

Visitors to Egypt enjoy riding camels.

Fast Facts

Capital city: Cairo

Population of Egypt:
More than 97 million

Main language:
Egyptian Arabic

Money:
Egyptian pound

Major religions:
Islam and Christianity

Neighboring countries: Libya, Sudan, and Israel

Cool Fact: The ancient Egyptians invented toothpaste!

Glossary

capital (KAP-uh-tul) the city where a country's government is based

civilizations (siv-il-eye-ZAY-shunz) ways of life of particular areas and groups of people

hieroglyphic (hye-ruh-GLIF-ik) belonging to a system of writing that uses pictures and symbols

revolution (rev-uh-LOO-shuhn) an uprising of people in a country that changes its government

tombs (TOOMZ) buildings or rooms for the dead

Index

Read More

Boyer, Crispin. *Everything Ancient Egypt.* Washington, DC: National Geographic (2012).

Heinrichs, Ann. *Egypt (Enchantment of the World).* New York: Scholastic (2012).

Learn More Online

To learn more about Egypt, visit
www.bearportpublishing.com/CountriesWeComeFrom

About the Author

Rachel Anne Cantor is a writer who lives
in Massachusetts. She loves learning
about Egypt's ancient history
and its modern culture.